Weather Encyclopedia

by Kevin Beals and Josey Baker

SEEDS OF SCIENCE
ROOTS OF READING®

Published and Distributed by
Delta Education
...because children learn by doing.®
A member of School Specialty Science

Published and Distributed by

Delta Education
...because children learn by doing.®

A member of School Specialty Science

These materials are based upon work partially supported by the National Science Foundation under grant numbers ESI-0242733 and ESI-0628272. The Federal Government has certain rights in this material. Any opinions, findings, and conclusions or recommendations expressed in this material are those of the author(s) and do not necessarily reflect the views of the National Science Foundation.

Developed at Lawrence Hall of Science and the Graduate School of Education at the University of California at Berkeley

Seeds of Science/Roots of Reading® is a collaboration of a science team led by Jacqueline Barber and a literacy team led by P. David Pearson and Gina Cervetti.

Delta Education LLC
PO Box 3000
Nashua, NH 03061
1-800-258-1302
www.deltaeducation.com

Weather Encyclopedia
594-0038
ISBN: 978-1-59821-512-0
Printing 1 – 10/2009
Standard Printing Company, Canton, OH

Contents

Atmosphere

Most **planets** are **surrounded** by a **mixture** of **gases**. The mixture of gases surrounding a planet is called an **atmosphere**. These gases stay near the **surface** of the planet because of gravity. Gravity pulls the gases toward the planet and keeps them from floating into space.

Earth's atmosphere surrounds the planet and reaches up about 350 miles into the sky. Earth has a very special atmosphere. It is made of air that living things can breathe. This air is made of gases such as **oxygen** and **nitrogen**. Earth's atmosphere is also special because it protects us from the harmful rays of the Sun and makes **weather** possible. Without this special atmosphere, most living things we know of could not **survive**.

See also: atmospheric pressure, meteorology, sunlight, water cycle

Layers of the Atmosphere

Earth's atmosphere is divided into four layers. The first layer is at the bottom, closest to the Earth's surface. It is the **troposphere**. The troposphere starts at the ground and reaches up to about nine miles above the ground. Most weather happens in the troposphere. The troposphere is sometimes called the lower atmosphere.

The second layer is the **stratosphere**. The stratosphere starts right above the troposphere. It ends about 30 miles above the ground. About 99 percent of all air is in the troposphere and stratosphere. As you go higher and higher in the stratosphere, there is less and less air.

The third layer is the **mesosphere**. The mesosphere starts right above the stratosphere and ends about 50 miles above the ground. The mesosphere is the coldest layer of the atmosphere.

The fourth layer is the **thermosphere**. The thermosphere starts right above the mesosphere and ends about 350 miles above the ground. No weather happens in the thermosphere or the mesosphere because those layers have very little air and no **water vapor**.

Earth's Atmosphere

Atmospheric Pressure

The **atmosphere** is the **mixture** of invisible **gases** **surrounding** Earth. We call this mixture air. Air is invisible, but we can feel it. Air has weight and takes up space. **Atmospheric pressure** is the weight of air pressing against us from all directions. Atmospheric pressure can be high or low, but we usually can't feel the difference. High atmospheric pressure means air is pressing harder. Low atmospheric pressure means air is not pressing as hard. In one area, the atmospheric pressure might be high sometimes and low at other times.

Meteorologists keep track of Highs (areas of high atmospheric pressure) and Lows (areas of low atmospheric pressure) because atmospheric pressure **affects** the **weather**. Highs usually mean clear skies and no rain. Lows often mean wet weather. When the atmospheric pressure is low, warm air rises and cools off. This causes **clouds**, **precipitation**, and storms. Weather maps often show atmospheric pressure with the letters *H* for High and *L* for Low.

See also: atmosphere, clouds, precipitation, weather maps, wind

Tool for Measuring Atmospheric Pressure

A **barometer** is a tool that **measures** atmospheric pressure. It measures how much the air above us is pressing on us. Barometers are used for **predicting** the weather. If a barometer shows that the atmospheric pressure is getting lower, wet weather might be coming. If the barometer shows atmospheric pressure is staying the same or getting higher, there will probably be clear skies.

Blizzards

Blizzards are powerful snowstorms with strong winds, low **temperatures**, and a lot of blowing snow. In many blizzards, falling snow is blown sideways by the wind. In some blizzards, the wind picks up snow that has already fallen and blows it around.

A snowstorm is not called a blizzard unless the blowing snow makes it impossible for people to see more than a quarter of a mile in front of them. The wind during a blizzard must blow at least 35 miles per hour, and the storm must last for at least three hours.

See also: snow, wind

Climate

Climate is the set of **weather conditions** that are normal for a place. This includes how much **precipitation** usually falls and when, the normal range of **temperatures**, the direction wind usually blows, and more. Different places may have different climates. For example, the climate in a desert is not like the climate in a **tropical** place. In some places, the climate includes a rainy season and a dry season. In other places, there is some precipitation throughout the year. Some climates include big changes in temperature from winter to summer.

Meteorologists investigate the climate in the places they study. Knowing about the climate helps meteorologists make **predictions**. Meteorologists keep track of weather **patterns** to see if they match what is normal for a place's climate. When a place has weather that is unusual, it can cause problems. For example, a **drought** occurs when a place gets much less rain than usual.

Meteorologists and other scientists have discovered that pollution is causing climates around the world to change. This might cause problems when people are not prepared for extreme weather changes, such as higher temperatures or more storms.

See also: drought, meteorology, precipitation, temperature

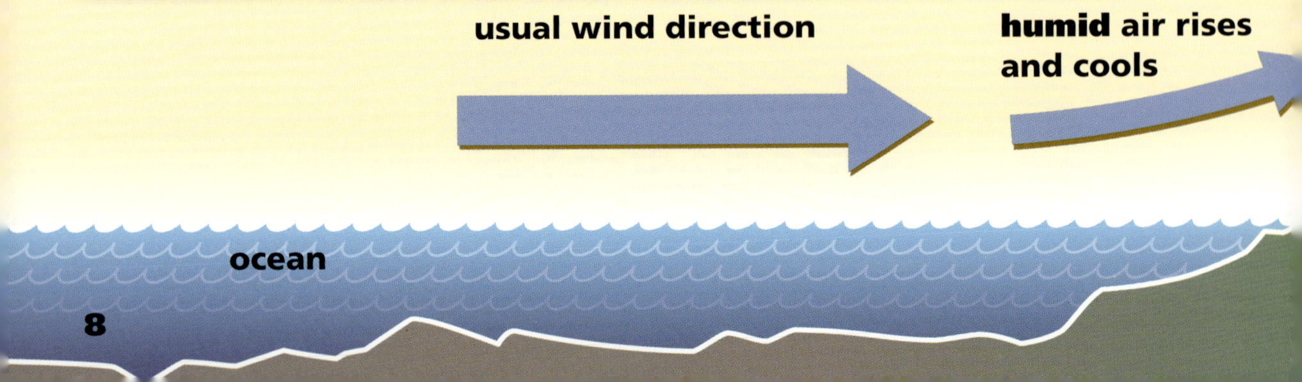

Did You Know?

Mountain ranges can **affect** the climate in nearby areas. If the wind usually blows in one direction, the side of the mountain range that is facing the wind may get a lot of precipitation. The other side of the mountain range may get very little. When the wind moves air to the mountains, the air gets pushed up higher in the **atmosphere** by the slope of the mountains. The air cools as it rises, and **water vapor** in the air **condenses**. Precipitation falls on the side of the mountain range that is facing the wind. By the time the air moves over the mountains, it has lost its **humidity**. The dry air doesn't bring as much precipitation.

Clouds

A **cloud** is a group of many tiny water **droplets** or ice **crystals** that stay up in the air. Clouds often form when warm air rises. As the warm air rises, it cools. Warm air can have more **water vapor** in it than cold air. When the warm air cools, some of the water vapor **condenses**. That means the water vapor turns into tiny water droplets. If the air is very cold, water vapor might change **phase** into ice crystals. The water droplets or ice crystals form on tiny pieces of **solids**, such as dust. The droplets and ice crystals are so small and light that the air holds them up. When billions of these droplets form in one part of the sky, they make a cloud.

Types of Clouds

There are many different types of clouds. Different types of clouds might bring different types of **weather**. Four of the most common clouds are **cumulus**, **stratus**, **cirrus**, and **nimbus**.

See also: condensation, fog, precipitation, temperature

Cumulus clouds look white and puffy, like cotton balls or popcorn. They are low-level or mid-level clouds. Cumulus clouds are usually made of water droplets, but when they get very tall they might be made of ice crystals. Cumulus clouds are sometimes called fair weather clouds because they often mean good weather. But if cumulus clouds get very tall, they can turn gray and bring rain, snow, or hailstorms. Some cumulus clouds might form **tornadoes**.

Stratus clouds are flat and stretch out over the sky like a blanket. They can be white or gray. Stratus clouds are usually low clouds, but some kinds can be mid-level or high-level. Stratus clouds are usually made of water droplets, but when they are very high they might be made of ice crystals. Stratus clouds might bring rain or snow. When stratus clouds form so close to the ground that they touch it, they are called **fog**.

Cirrus clouds are found very high in the sky, usually at least five miles up. Because it is very cold so high up, these clouds are made of ice crystals. Cirrus clouds look thin, white, and feathery.

The word *nimbus* is used in cloud names to describe rain clouds. A cumulonimbus cloud is a cumulus rain cloud. A nimbostratus cloud is a stratus rain cloud.

Condensation

Condensation is when a **gas** turns into a **liquid**. An example of condensation is when **water vapor** turns into liquid water. Water vapor is the name for water in its gas **phase**.

There is water vapor in air. If the air cools, some of the water vapor might **condense** into **droplets** of liquid water. When this happens, **clouds**, **fog**, or **dew** might form. Water vapor in the air might condense into liquid droplets when it hits something cold, such as a cold window or a cold juice can.

The **temperature** at which condensation happens is called the dew point. There is no one temperature at which condensation happens. The dew point is different under different **conditions**. For example, dew point depends on temperature and **humidity**.

See also: clouds, dew, humidity, temperature, water cycle

Dew

Dew is **liquid** water that forms on the ground or on **objects** such as grass, leaves, cars, and spiderwebs. Dew starts as **water vapor** in the air. After the Sun sets, the ground gets colder and so do objects near the ground. Because of this cooling, some water vapor in the air **condenses** into liquid water. The tiny drops of liquid water form on the ground or on objects.

These water **droplets** are dew. The dew makes things look and feel wet in the morning. Dew doesn't necessarily form every night. The ground or object has to get cold enough and the air has to be **humid** enough. The tiny droplets of water that form on the outside of a glass of cold liquid are also a form of dew. The cold makes the water vapor condense out of the air into droplets of liquid water on the outside of the glass.

See also: condensation, frost, humidity

Drought

Droughts happen when there is less **precipitation** than normal for a **climate** over a long time. Droughts are a natural part of **weather**. Droughts might cause problems if there is not enough water for things such as watering plants or drinking. During a drought, streams might dry up and plants might die.

Changes in ordinary weather **patterns** can cause drought. For example, winds that blow in different directions than usual might keep rainstorms away from an area. Some places depend on **melted** snow from faraway mountains for water. In those places, droughts might happen when less snow falls on the mountains than usual.

See also: climate, precipitation, rain, snow, wind

Evaporation

Evaporation is when a **liquid** turns into a **gas**. One example of this is when liquid water turns into **water vapor** in the air. Water vapor is the name for water in its gas **phase**. Evaporation is the opposite of **condensation**, which is when a gas turns into a liquid.

Evaporation only happens at the **surface** of the liquid. Water at the surface of a drop, puddle, lake, or other body of water is touching air. Heat makes the water at the surface turn into water vapor that goes into the air. Water that is not at the surface cannot break away into the air.

Evaporation happens faster with hotter **temperatures**. On a hot day, a puddle will **evaporate** more quickly than on a cold day.

Moving air also speeds up evaporation. A puddle will evaporate more quickly on a windy day than it will on a day with no wind. On a hot and windy day, water will evaporate very quickly.

Another thing that can make evaporation happen faster is low **humidity**. Air that is not very **humid** does not have much water vapor in it. This air can hold a lot more water vapor, so evaporation can happen quickly. Evaporation happens fastest in very dry places, such as deserts.

Evaporation is an important part of the **water cycle**. All the water vapor in the air is there because it evaporated from liquid water.

See also: humidity, temperature, water cycle

Did You Know?

If water gets hot enough, it boils. When water boils, bubbles of water vapor float to the surface. That's because liquid water below the surface is changing to water vapor. But boiling is not the same as evaporation. Evaporation only happens at the water's surface, and boiling happens below the surface. Water can only boil when its temperature is above 212°F (**degrees** Fahrenheit). Evaporation can happen at any temperature. Even at cold temperatures, evaporation is happening—just very slowly.

Floods

During a flood, land that is usually dry becomes covered with water. It could just be an inch of water, or it could be a hundred feet! Floods can happen for many different reasons. Too much rain can cause a flood. A flood might happen if a lot of snow **melts** very fast. Big storms in or near the ocean can also cause floods.

A flood that happens very fast is called a flash flood. Flash floods can happen if it rains very hard in a short period of time. There is no time for the ground to soak up all the water, and the water flows over the ground. Flash floods are dangerous because they can happen suddenly, without any warning.

See also: groundwater, rain, runoff, snow

Fog

Fog is a **stratus cloud** that stays near the ground. When warm, wet air cools, the **water vapor** in the air **condenses** to form water **droplets**. The droplets form on tiny pieces of **solid** stuff in the air, such as dust. The droplets are so small that the air holds them up. These billions of water droplets together form fog (if they are close to the ground) or a cloud (if they are up in the air).

Fog forms when warm air gets cooler near the ground. This sometimes happens in the morning after a cold night, as the air cools near the cold ground. Fog can also form when warm air passes over cold water, such as a lake or the ocean. Sometimes, fog forms when a warm breeze moves up a mountain. As the air moves higher and higher, it cools. As the air cools, water vapor condenses out of the air, forming fog.

See also: clouds, condensation

Freezing Rain

Freezing rain falls as **liquid** water, but it **freezes** as soon as it hits the ground. Freezing rain can cover everything it hits with a very slippery layer of ice. When freezing rain falls, this type of **weather** is called an ice storm.

Freezing rain forms when **precipitation** falls through layers of warm and cold air high above the ground. First, snow falls through warm air, **melting** into liquid rain. Then this liquid rain falls through air that is colder than **freezing temperature**, or 32°F (**degrees** Fahrenheit). But the rain doesn't freeze. Instead, it turns into what is called **supercooled** liquid water. It is water that is below freezing temperature, but it is still liquid. When this supercooled water hits the ground, it immediately turns to ice.

People sometimes confuse freezing rain with other kinds of precipitation, such as sleet. Sleet is rain that has frozen high in the air. **Hail** and snow are two other kinds of precipitation made of **solid** frozen water. These kinds of precipitation are all different from freezing rain. Freezing rain is the only kind of precipitation that falls as liquid but then freezes as soon as it hits the ground.

See also: clouds, hail, precipitation, rain, sleet, snow

Frost

Frost is **water vapor** that changes **phase** into ice **crystals** on **solid surfaces**, such as plants and windows. Water vapor is water that is in its **gas** phase. There is a great deal of water vapor in the air. Frost is similar to **dew** in that it appears on cool surfaces near the ground, but frost forms only when the **temperature** of the ground is colder than **freezing**, or 32°F (**degrees** Fahrenheit).

When water vapor is cooled, it often **condenses** into **liquid** water. This is how dew forms. This liquid water might later **freeze** into solid ice. But when frost forms, it skips the liquid phase. The water vapor turns directly into solid ice without first becoming liquid.

See also: dew, temperature

Groundwater

Groundwater is freshwater found in the soil and rock under the Earth's **surface**. The spaces underground where groundwater collects are similar to the holes of a sponge.

Groundwater is important because it is a source of freshwater for people to drink. Half of the people in the United States get some or all of their drinking water from groundwater. Farmers also use groundwater to water their crops. People dig wells to reach groundwater, and then a **pump** brings the water to the surface. Groundwater can also be close to the surface. **Seeps** or **springs** are the places where groundwater comes to the surface naturally.

See also: runoff, water cycle

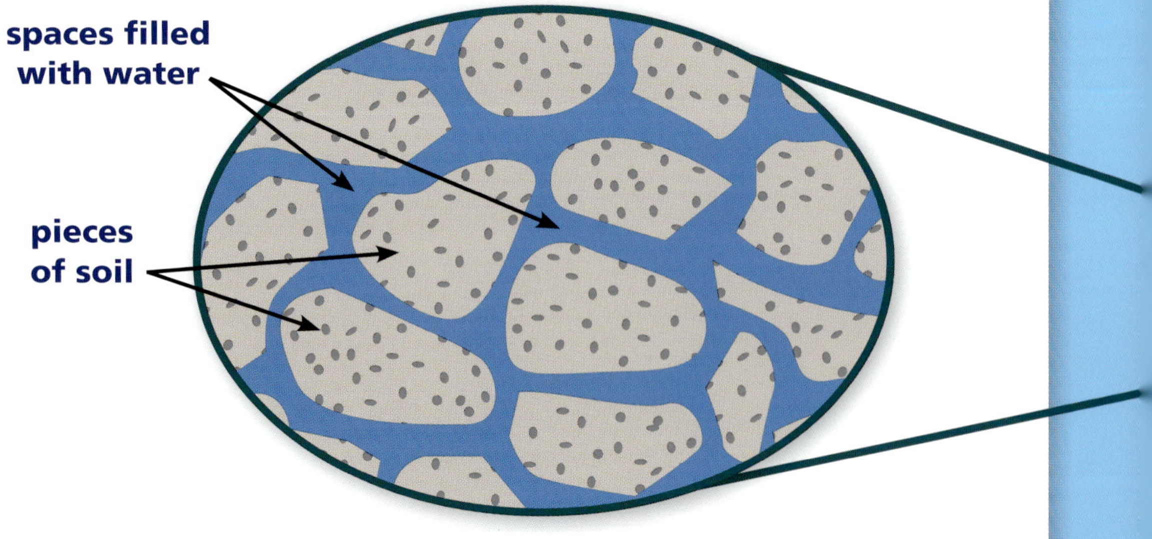

The spaces in this soil are filled with groundwater.

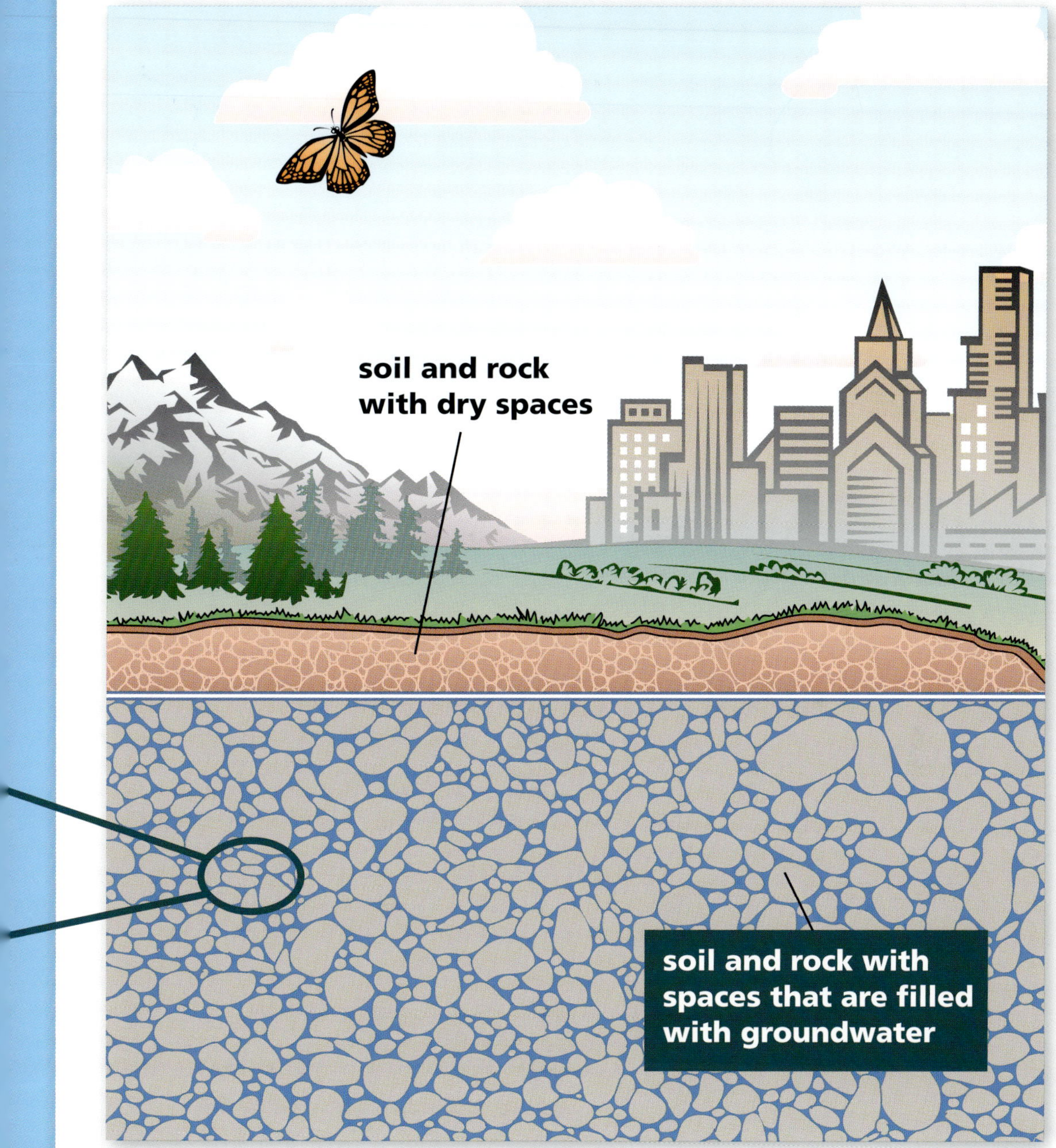
soil and rock
with dry spaces
soil and rock with
spaces that are filled
with groundwater

Hail

Hail is a kind of **precipitation** that can fall during storms, especially **thunderstorms**. **Hailstones** are made of frozen water. Hailstones are hard balls of ice that form in **clouds** on specks of dust, sand, dirt, ash, or even tiny insects.

Hailstorms have strong winds that blow in all directions. Sometimes, wind blows raindrops straight up to the top of a storm cloud, where the air is colder than **freezing**, or 32°F (**degrees** Fahrenheit). At the top of the storm cloud, the raindrops **freeze** into ice. Strong winds blowing upward keep these frozen raindrops **hovering** high in the storm cloud. As each frozen raindrop hovers, new raindrops blow upward and hit the frozen raindrop. When new **liquid** raindrops hit the frozen raindrop, the liquid raindrops freeze. This covers the frozen raindrop with a new layer of ice. When enough layers build up, the frozen raindrop becomes large enough to be called a hailstone.

The longer a hailstone stays high in the storm cloud, the more layers of ice will build up on it. The layers of ice make the hailstone bigger. Once the hailstone is too heavy for the wind to hold up, it falls to the ground. Hailstones are often small, but some can grow very large.

Hail is different from snow, snowflakes, sleet, and freezing rain. Hail and sleet are similar, but they are not the same. Sleet is rain that has frozen on its way to the ground. Hail freezes into balls before it even falls from the sky.

See also: clouds, precipitation, sleet, thunderstorms

Did You Know?

A hailstone can grow as big as a softball! When giant hail falls from the sky, car windshields and roofs of houses can be damaged. Holes in the ground left by the impact of these stones can be a foot across. The heaviest hailstone ever to fall in the United States weighed one and a half pounds. The largest hailstone didn't weigh as much but was almost 19 inches around.

Humidity

Humidity is a **measurement** of how much **water vapor** is in the air. Water vapor is **liquid** water that has **evaporated** into the air. Water vapor is invisible—you can't see it at all. When you see tiny **droplets** of water, such as **fog**, **clouds**, or the mist above a teapot, you are seeing liquid water, *not* water vapor.

(CONTINUED)

Some people find that their hair curls more on humid days.

Humidity (CONTINUED)

Humidity is different in different parts of the world. For example, the air in the eastern part of the United States is usually more **humid** than the air in the western part. Air above a lake or the ocean is likely to be more humid than air in other places. Water from the lake or ocean evaporates into the air, making the air more humid.

Humidity in a place can change from day to day. **Meteorologists measure** humidity in order to help **predict** the **weather**. Air often becomes more humid before rain or snow falls.

Warm air can usually hold more water vapor than cold air. Places that have hot **temperatures** and are near the ocean often have very high humidity. However, not all hot places have high humidity. Deserts have low humidity, even though they can be very hot.

See also: climate, condensation, evaporation, temperature

Did You Know?

High or low humidity can make people feel very uncomfortable. When we sweat, our bodies are using the **evaporation** of the water in our sweat to cool us off. When humidity is high, sweat evaporates very slowly. This can make people feel hot, sticky, and uncomfortable. Low humidity can feel uncomfortable, too. Water evaporates fast when humidity is low, and that can make people's skin very dry.

Tool for Measuring Humidity

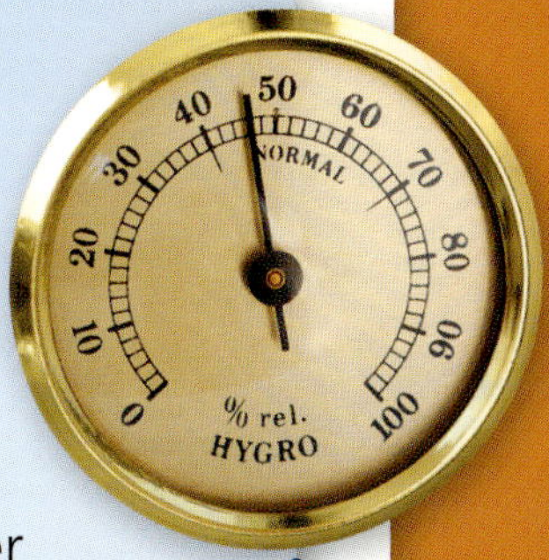

A **hygrometer** is a tool that measures humidity on a scale from 0 to 100. Lower numbers mean the humidity is lower, and higher numbers mean the humidity is higher. When humidity is at 100, the air can't hold any more water vapor. When it is this humid, the water vapor **condenses** to liquid water droplets, forming clouds and sometimes causing rain. But humidity is often different at ground level than it is high above the ground. For example, the humidity might be 100 up where the clouds are, and it might be 87 down near the ground. That's why rain might fall even at times when a hygrometer on the ground is measuring humidity of less than 100.

Hurricanes

Hurricanes are huge, swirling storms that start over warm ocean waters. To be a hurricane, the storm must have winds of 74 miles per hour or faster. Wind in a hurricane can be as fast as 200 miles per hour! Hurricanes bring huge amounts of rain. They can also cause **tornadoes**, large ocean waves, and floods. Hurricanes can last for days or even weeks, and they can be very dangerous.

A hurricane usually starts from a group of smaller **thunderstorms** in **humid** air above warm ocean water. Most hurricanes happen in late summer and early fall, when ocean water is warmest. Thunderstorms start when the warm water **evaporates** and becomes **water vapor**. The water vapor rises into the **atmosphere**. The water vapor gets colder as it rises and so it **condenses**. This forms tall **cumulus** thunderclouds. Wind can cause these thunderclouds to spin. As a group of storm **clouds** spins, it gathers more warm, humid air, and the clouds get bigger. The winds become more powerful. When a hurricane moves over land, or over cold water, it loses strength. Without warm water below it, a hurricane can't keep gathering humid air.

Meteorologists carefully **observe** storms over the ocean. These **weather** scientists notice hurricanes forming and keep track of where they move. Meteorologists then make **predictions** of where and when hurricanes will reach land. These predictions are used to warn people about the dangers of the wind, rain, and waves from the hurricane.

See also: meteorology, thunderstorms, wind

Lightning

Lightning is a huge electric spark in the **atmosphere**. Electric sparks can only flow through the air when electric forces are very strong. These strong electric forces build up when air, water drops, and pieces of ice rub against one another in the atmosphere. This often happens in cumulonimbus **clouds**, where strong **gusts** of wind move air, ice, and water drops around. Storms with lightning are called **thunderstorms**.

Lightning can strike inside a cloud, or it can go from one cloud to another. Lightning can also strike from a cloud to the ground or to an **object** on the ground. Objects on Earth are more likely to be hit by lightning if they are higher than other objects around them.

See also: clouds, thunderstorms

Did You Know?

- Lightning strikes somewhere in the world about twice every three seconds.
- A bolt of lightning heats the air very quickly to many thousands of **degrees** Fahrenheit. The sudden rise in **temperature** sends **vibrations** through the air, and these vibrations are heard as thunder.

Meteorology

Meteorology is the study of the **atmosphere** and **weather**. Weather **affects** everyone, so there are many people around the world who study meteorology. Scientists who study weather are called **meteorologists**.

It is difficult to **predict** the weather because there are so many things to **consider**. For example, wind speed, **temperature**, and **cloud** formations all affect the weather. Meteorologists use computers and math to help them look at all these different things at one time. This helps them make more accurate **predictions**.

Meteorologists also collect **data** using weather stations and tools such as weather balloons and planes. They use this data to make weather maps. Weather maps help meteorologists predict and report the weather.

Meteorologists use sky **observations** to describe the weather and predict whether **precipitation** will fall. They often **observe** the sky using pictures of Earth taken from **satellites** in space. With these pictures, they can look *down* at clouds instead of up at them!

Meteorologists use the following words to describe the amount of cloud cover in the sky:

- clear (no clouds or almost no clouds)
- partly cloudy (some clouds and some clear sky)
- mostly cloudy (most of the sky covered by clouds, with a little bit of clear sky)
- **overcast** (all of the sky covered by clouds)
- foggy (clouds at or near ground level)

See also: atmosphere, climate, clouds, weather maps

Did You Know?

Many people think of meteorologists as people on television who give weather forecasts. This is only one kind of meteorologist, and there are many other kinds. Some meteorologists work for the government, others work for farmers, and still others work in labs.

Kind of Precipitation

snow

rain

sleet

freezing rain

hail

Precipitation

Precipitation is **solid** or **liquid** water that falls to Earth. There are many different kinds of precipitation.

Precipitation happens when enough **water vapor** changes **phase** to form water **droplets** or ice **crystals** in the air. These droplets or ice crystals form **clouds**.

When water droplets or ice crystals touch other water droplets or ice crystals, they might join together. If many droplets or crystals join together, they form water drops or snowflakes. When water drops or snowflakes get big enough, they become too heavy to stay up in a cloud. They fall to Earth as precipitation. Depending on how cold the air **temperatures** are, precipitation might fall as rain, snow, freezing rain, sleet, or **hail**.

Precipitation is an important part of the **water cycle**. Precipitation brings water from the **atmosphere** back down to the Earth's **surface**.

See also: climate, clouds, freezing rain, hail, rain, sleet, snow, water cycle

Rain

Rain is a kind of **precipitation** that forms in **clouds** and falls to Earth as drops of water. Clouds often form when **water vapor condenses** out of the air into tiny **liquid** water **droplets** or turns into tiny ice **crystals**. The water droplets or ice crystals are so light that they stay up in the air. When enough of them come together, a cloud forms. When the droplets bump into other droplets, they might make bigger drops. When the drops get heavy enough, they fall as rain.

Sometimes, rain starts out as ice crystals. If ice crystals fall from a cloud and pass through warmer air below, they may **melt**. If this happens, they hit the ground as liquid rain.

See also: climate, clouds, drought, floods, precipitation

Tool for Measuring Rain

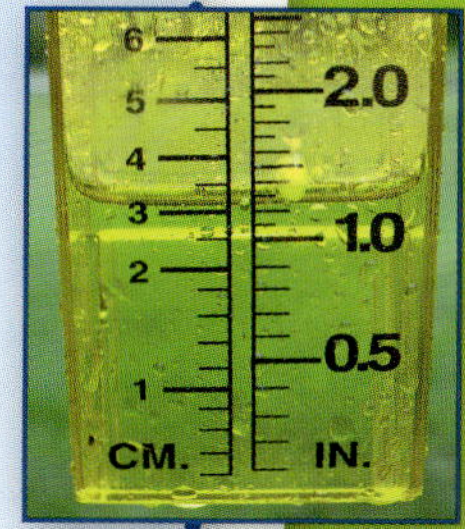

A **rain gauge** is a tool that collects and **measures** rain. The rain may be measured in inches, millimeters, or centimeters. **Meteorologists** use rain gauges to know how much rain has fallen in a day, a month, or a year. This can help them **predict** and understand floods and **droughts**. By keeping track of rainfall in one place over time, meteorologists figure out what is a normal amount of rain for that place to get in a year or in a season. They notice whether the amount of rain that is falling in a year is normal, more than normal, or less than normal.

Runoff

Runoff is a part of the **water cycle**. After **precipitation** such as rain or snow falls to Earth, some of the water might flow downhill over the ground. The movement of water over the land is called runoff. This includes water moving in rivers and streams. Rivers and streams usually flow into lakes and the ocean.

Not all precipitation becomes runoff. A lot of the water that falls from the sky soaks into the ground to become **groundwater**. When rain falls on dry ground, there is not much runoff because most of the water soaks into the ground. But wet ground might become so full of water that it can't hold any more. When rain falls on wet ground, there might be a lot of runoff, or even floods. There might also be lots of runoff in places where the ground is covered with roads, parking lots, and sidewalks. In these places, water can't soak into the ground.

See also: floods, groundwater, precipitation, water cycle

Sleet

Sleet is a type of **precipitation**. Sleet can start as rain or snow. When a raindrop or snowflake falls through the sky, it passes through many different layers of air. Some layers are warm, and some are cold. Sometimes, a snowflake **melts** when it passes through a warm layer of air. But it might **freeze** again when it passes through a cold layer. Snowflakes that melt and then freeze again before they fall to the ground are called sleet. Raindrops that freeze on their way to the ground are also called sleet.

Although it is frozen water, sleet is different from snow or **hail**. Both snow and hail form in **clouds**. But sleet is raindrops or melted snowflakes that have frozen into ice on their way down to the ground. Sleet is usually smaller than hail.

Sleet is also different from freezing rain. Freezing rain falls as **supercooled liquid** water and then freezes as soon as it hits the ground.

See also: clouds, freezing rain, hail, precipitation, rain, snow

Snow

Snow is a kind of **precipitation** that is made of **solid** water **crystals**. For snow to fall, the air in a **cloud** must have a lot of **water vapor** in it, and the **temperature** must be below **freezing**, or 32°F (**degrees** Fahrenheit). Most snow forms when water vapor turns directly into ice crystals without first becoming **liquid** water. This happens in the clouds.

Snow crystals form on tiny **objects** in the air, such as dust. As the crystals grow, snowflake **patterns** form. The crystals grow bigger until they are big enough to fall from the clouds. As they fall, they smash into one another. Parts of the crystals might **melt** and refreeze. A snowflake that reaches the ground might have pieces of thousands of ice crystals in it.

When a lot of snow falls, it's called a snowstorm. A **blizzard** is a snowstorm with strong winds and heavy snow.

See also: blizzards, climate, clouds, drought, floods, precipitation

Did You Know?

- Some people think that snow is made of frozen raindrops, but it's not. Raindrops are made of liquid water. If raindrops **freeze** on their way to the ground, they are called sleet.
- Snow piles up quickly. The same amount of water that makes one inch of rain can make eight inches of snow!

Sunlight

The Sun makes the **water cycle** and Earth's **weather** happen. Sunlight warms up water in the ocean, lakes, rivers, and the ground. This makes some of the water **evaporate**. When **liquid** water evaporates, it becomes **water vapor** in the air. Sunlight also warms the air in the **atmosphere**. The warm air rises, carrying water vapor with it. Without this rising water vapor, there would be no water cycle.

Sunlight also causes different kinds of weather. Sunlight makes Earth warmer in some places than in others. For example, sunlight generally heats up land faster than it heats up the ocean. In warmer areas, the warm air rises up high in the atmosphere and moves toward areas where the air is colder. In colder areas, the cold air stays low and moves toward warmer areas. These movements of air cause wind. When warm and cold air meet, **precipitation**, storms, and other kinds of weather happen in the atmosphere.

See also: evaporation, temperature, water cycle, wind

Temperature

When **meteorologists** talk about **temperature**, they are usually talking about air temperature—how hot or cold the air is. Temperature is an important part of **weather**. The temperature of air **affects** how much **water vapor** the air can hold. When air cools, water vapor in the air might **condense** into **liquid droplets** to form **clouds**. Warmer temperatures might make clouds **evaporate**.

Whether water is liquid, **solid** (ice), or **gas** (water vapor) partly depends on the temperature of the water. Usually, the higher the temperature is, the faster liquid water will evaporate to form water vapor. Usually, the lower the temperature is, the faster water vapor will condense into liquid water. If the temperature drops below **freezing**, or 32°F (**degrees** Fahrenheit), the water can **freeze** to form solid ice.

Temperature affects whether **precipitation** falls as rain, snow, sleet, **hail**, or freezing rain. The temperature at ground level is important, but so is the temperature in the clouds where the precipitation is formed. It's also important to know the temperature of the air that the precipitation falls through, because the precipitation may freeze or **melt** on its way down. **Measuring** the temperature at different heights in the **atmosphere** helps meteorologists **predict** what kind of precipitation might fall.

See also: climate, condensation, evaporation, humidity, meteorology, sunlight

Tool for Measuring Temperature

A **thermometer** is a tool meteorologists use to measure the temperature of the air. Temperature can be measured in Fahrenheit or Celsius. These **measurements** are two different temperature scales, so the same temperature will have a different number in Fahrenheit and Celsius. For example, freezing temperature is 32°F (degrees Fahrenheit), but it's 0°C (degrees Celsius).

When meteorologists measure temperature, they measure it in the shade—not in the sunlight. This is because they want to measure how warm the *air* is. If sunlight hits the thermometer, the sunlight will make the thermometer warmer than the air.

This thermometer shows the temperature is 77°F, or 25°C.

Thunderstorms

All **thunderstorms** make lightning. Thunder is the sound lightning makes when the lightning heats up the air very quickly. Whenever there is thunder, there is lightning, too. Most thunderstorms also have heavy rains and winds. These storms are usually from 30 minutes to an hour long, but some thunderstorms can last for hours. These storms could have **hail**, snow, or even **tornadoes**. Lightning can hit people, and it can also cause fires. Heavy rains from thunderstorms can cause flash floods.

Thunderstorms form in warm, **humid weather**, usually in spring or summer. When the warm, moist air rises, **water vapor** in the air **condenses** into **droplets** of **liquid** water. These droplets form puffy, white **clouds** called **cumulus** clouds. If the clouds keep growing, they can turn into cumulonimbus clouds. Cumulonimbus clouds are tall, dark, puffy clouds. Cumulonimbus clouds are sometimes called thunderheads because lightning and thunder might form inside them. Strong **gusts** of wind blow water drops and ice around inside the cumulonimbus clouds. When the ice or water drops become too heavy, they fall out of the cloud as rain, hail, or sometimes snow.

See also: clouds, floods, hail, lightning, rain, tornadoes

Tornadoes

A **tornado** is a spinning tube of air that reaches from a thundercloud to the ground. It looks like a large funnel hanging down from storm **clouds**. Wind inside a tornado can be as fast as 300 miles per hour! Tornadoes most often happen in the United States and can happen at any time of the year.

Tornadoes come from **thunderstorms**, but not all thunderstorms cause tornadoes. To make tornadoes, a storm must have very tall clouds and **humid** air. A tornado can form when the wind at different heights in a storm is blowing at different speeds or in different directions. When a thunderstorm starts to spin, it might create one or more tornadoes.

Tornadoes are very dangerous. Their winds are so strong that they can tear buildings apart, break trees, and flip cars. Unlike other kinds of extreme **weather**, most tornadoes last only a short time—less than 20 minutes—and travel only a short distance. **Meteorologists** work hard to **predict** tornadoes so that people can protect themselves. It is difficult to predict tornadoes, however, and people sometimes get only 15 minutes of warning before a tornado hits.

See also: humidity, meteorology, thunderstorms, wind

Water Cycle

The **water cycle** is the movement of water in and between the **atmosphere**, the **surface** of the Earth, and underground. There is no beginning or end to the water cycle. The water keeps getting **recycled** through the atmosphere, the surface of the Earth, and underground, over and over again! The Sun drives the water cycle by changing the **phase** of water from **solid** to **liquid** to **gas**. Without the heat from the Sun, the water on Earth would not change phase—it would all be solid ice!

The stages of the water cycle are evaporation, condensation, precipitation, and runoff.

Stages of the Water Cycle

Water goes through different stages in the water cycle:

Evaporation: Water that is on the ground or in the ocean heats up and ***evaporates*** into **water vapor** in the air. The air rises up into the atmosphere, carrying the water vapor with it.

Condensation: As the water vapor rises, it cools. This might cause it to ***condense*** into **droplets** of liquid water. If the air is cold enough, the water vapor can change phase to become solid ice **crystals** instead. The water droplets or ice crystals are so small that the air holds them up. This is how a **cloud** forms.

Precipitation: Water droplets or ice crystals in a cloud can bump into one another and stick together. These bigger, heavier drops or crystals fall to the ground as ***precipitation***.

Runoff: Once the precipitation reaches the ground, it might flow over the land in rivers and streams. The movement of water over the surface of the Earth is called ***runoff***. This water eventually evaporates again, continuing the **cycle**.

Water also moves through the water cycle in other ways. A lot of precipitation soaks into the ground and slowly moves under the ground. This is called **groundwater**. When water from runoff stops flowing, it collects in lakes and the ocean. This water also evaporates eventually and moves again through the water cycle.

See also: atmosphere, condensation, evaporation, groundwater, precipitation, runoff, sunlight

Weather Maps

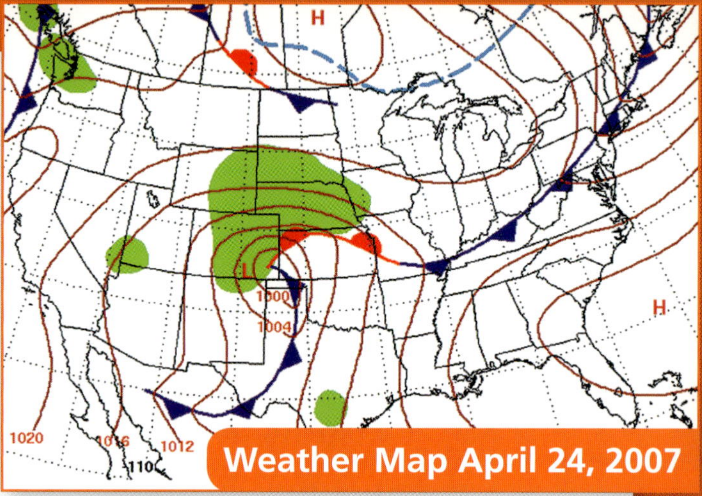

Weather Map April 24, 2007

Weather maps show what the weather is like in one area at one time. Some weather maps have information about **temperature**, **cloud** cover, **precipitation**, **atmospheric pressure**, or wind direction.

Weather maps use **symbols**, colors, and numbers to show **data**. On some weather maps, an *H* stands for High pressure, which usually means clear weather. An *L* stands for Low pressure, which usually means precipitation. A line of blue triangles shows cold air moving across the map. The triangles point in the direction the cold air is moving. A line of red half-circles shows warm air moving across the map. The half-circles point in the direction the warm air is moving. (A line with blue triangles and red half-circles mixed together has warm air on one side and cold air on the other, and the air is not moving much.)

Weather maps often have keys or legends that show what the symbols, colors, and numbers stand for. They also usually have titles that tell the date and what the map shows.

Meteorologists make and use weather maps to help them **predict** the weather.

See also: atmospheric pressure, meteorology, precipitation, temperature, wind

Wind

Wind is air that moves from one place to another. Wind is caused by differences in **atmospheric pressure**. When sunlight warms air, the air rises, creating an area of low atmospheric pressure. Wind is usually air moving from an area of high atmospheric pressure to an area of low atmospheric pressure. The wind speeds up when there is a bigger difference in atmospheric pressure.

Without wind, the **weather** would not change very much. Wind brings weather to an area. If you know there is a storm near where you live, and there is wind coming from that direction, you might **predict** that the storm will hit your area. If there is clear weather near where you live, and the wind is coming from that direction, then you might predict clear weather. If wind is coming from across an ocean or a big lake, the wind might bring **humid** air.

Meteorologists usually explain wind by naming its speed and direction. Meteorologists **measure** wind direction because it helps them predict the weather for the next few days. When meteorologists talk about wind direction, they are talking about where the wind is coming from. For example, if a meteorologist talks about a north wind (or a northerly wind), that wind is blowing from the north. If a wind is coming from the southwest instead, it is called a southwest wind.

See also: atmospheric pressure, blizzards, hurricanes, sunlight, tornadoes, weather maps

(CONTINUED)

Tools for Measuring Wind

An **anemometer** is a tool used to measure wind speed. Knowing the wind speed helps meteorologists predict how quickly new weather will arrive. It also helps them know how dangerous storms, **hurricanes**, and **tornadoes** might be. Meteorologists also use anemometers to find places where the wind is almost always strong. These are the best places to build wind turbines.

A weather vane, also called a wind vane, is a tool that measures wind direction. Weather vanes are usually placed on roofs. Weather vanes balance on a point so that the wind can blow them around in a circle. A weather vane usually has an arrow that points in the direction the wind is coming from.

anemometer

wind turbines

weather vane

Glossary

affect: to change something

anemometer: a tool that measures wind speed

atmosphere: the air that surrounds Earth

atmospheric pressure: the force of the atmosphere pressing on something

barometer: a tool that measures atmospheric pressure

blizzard: a storm with fast winds and a lot of snow

cirrus: high clouds that are often feathery and are made of ice crystals

climate: the usual weather patterns in an area

cloud: water droplets or ice particles floating in the atmosphere

condensation: when a gas turns into a liquid

condense: to turn from a gas into a liquid

condition: what it is like in a certain place

consider: to think about

crystal: a substance with sharp edges and flat sides, like a diamond

cumulus: clouds that have flat bottoms and rounded popcorn-like tops, and are mostly made of water droplets

cycle: a series of events that happen over and over again

data: information collected in an investigation

degree: a measure of how hot or cold something is

dew: droplets of water that condense on plants or the ground

droplet: a tiny amount of water, smaller than a raindrop

drought: a time when there is much less precipitation than normal

evaporate: to turn from a liquid into a gas

evaporation: when a liquid turns into a gas

fog: a cloud that forms close to the ground

freeze: to turn from a liquid into a solid

freezing: the temperature at which water freezes into ice: 32°F (degrees Fahrenheit)

gas: a substance that is usually invisible, doesn't hold its shape, and spreads around, like air

groundwater: water that moves through soil underground

gust: a short burst of strong wind

hail: balls of ice that fall from storm clouds

hailstone: a single ball of ice that falls from a storm cloud

hover: to float in the air in one spot

humid: having lots of water vapor

humidity: the amount of water vapor in the air

hurricane: a huge, swirling storm that forms over warm ocean water

hygrometer: a tool for measuring humidity

investigate: to study or try to learn more about something

liquid: something that flows, doesn't hold its shape, and makes puddles, like water

measure: to use a tool to find information, such as how heavy, how big, how fast, or how hot or cold something is

measurement: a number that gives information about something, such as how heavy, how big, how fast, or how hot or cold it is

melt: to turn from a solid into a liquid

meteorologist: a scientist who studies weather

mixture: two or more substances mixed together

nimbus: a rain cloud

nitrogen: an invisible gas in the air

object: a thing that can be seen or touched

observation: information that you gather with your five senses

observe: to use any of the five senses to gather information about something

overcast: covered with clouds

oxygen: an invisible gas in the air, which people need to breathe

pattern: something that repeats or happens in a predictable way

phase: the form water or another substance takes, including solid, liquid, and gas

planet: a large, ball-shaped object that orbits a star

precipitation: liquid or solid water that falls to Earth

predict: to make a guess about what will happen, based on evidence

prediction: a guess about what will happen, based on evidence

pump: a machine that moves water upward

rain gauge: a tool for measuring how much rain has fallen

recycle: to go through a cycle again

runoff: the movement of liquid water across the land, such as in rivers and streams

satellite: a spacecraft with no people inside that circles Earth

seep: a place where groundwater comes up to the Earth's surface

solid: a substance that holds its shape and doesn't make puddles, like rock or wood

spring: a place where groundwater comes to the Earth's surface

stratus: low clouds that are shaped like flat gray layers, and are mostly made of water droplets

supercooled: at a temperature below freezing, but still liquid

surface: the top or outside of something

surround: to be all around something

survive: to stay alive

symbol: a picture that stands for something, such as a picture of a snowflake that stands for snow falling

temperature: how hot or cold something is

thermometer: a tool for measuring the temperature

thunderstorm: a storm with thunder and lightning

tornado: a tube of spinning air that reaches from a storm cloud to the ground

tropical: always hot and humid

vibration: fast movement back and forth

water cycle: the movement of water between Earth and the atmosphere

water vapor: water in the form of invisible gas

weather: what is happening with heat, water, and air in the lower atmosphere

Index